TEACHING

APPLIED PRINCIPLES OF LEARNING SERIES

WITH STYLE

Dr. Bruce H. Wilkinson

**Transform Your
Student's Attentiveness
and Your Effectiveness**

Teaching with Style
Course Workbook

Contents

Teaching with Style

A *Walk Thru the Bible Classic!*

A *"classic"* is something that has been around for a while, is highly esteemed for its value, and has had a long-standing impact in people's lives.

With that being the case, *Teaching With Style* certainly qualifies as a classic. For two decades, this series has changed the way teachers and facilitators understand and approach their teaching. And many lives—both students and teachers—have been changed as well!

Teaching With Style along with the other two titles in the Walk Thru the Bible teaching collection—*The 7 Laws of the Learner* and *The 7 Laws of the Teacher*—has equipped teachers in over 85 countries around the world!

Although the look of the video may be a bit dated, the material is just as relevant today as when the series was first introduced by Bruce Wilkinson. The challenges encountered by today's teachers are daunting. They are faced with issues like teaching in a world inundated with technology, constant changes in our knowledge base, global and economic information overload, and a multitude of distractions. It's a challenge to be an effective and engaging teacher with all that competition for student's attention! But Walk Thru the Bible can help! *Teaching With Style* is the answer to an age-old question—how to teach so that students are engaged, excited, and ready to learn!

We are pleased that you have joined us for a transformational experience! When you've completed *Teaching With Style*, be sure to check out the other two modules in our teaching series. Your teaching will never be the same! You can learn more on our website at www.walkthru.org/teachingseries.org.

About Walk Thru the Bible

Walk Thru the Bible ignites a passion for God's Word through innovative live events, inspiring biblical resources, and a global impact that changes lives worldwide… including yours.

Known for innovative methods and high-quality resources, we serve the whole body of Christ across denominational, cultural, and national lines. We partner with the local church worldwide to fulfill its mission, communicating the truths of God's Word in a way that makes the Bible readily accessible to anyone. Through our strong international network, we are strategically positioned to address the church's greatest need: developing mature, committed, and spiritually reproducing believers.

Our live events and small-group curricula are taught in more than 45 languages by more than 80,000 people in more than 85 countries, and more than 100 million devotionals have been packaged into daily magazines, books, and other publications that reach over five million people each year. Wherever you are on your journey, we can help.

Learn more about our global impact, Bibles, daily devotionals, small group curriculum, live events, and other resources at www.walkthru.org or call 1-800-361-6131.

WALK THRU THE BIBLE®

TAKE A WALK. CHANGE THE WORLD.

Transform Your Teaching!

ACSI Accredited CEU Courses!

Whether you are a professional teacher, a Sunday school teacher, a parent or a pastor, your teaching ability and effectiveness will be transformed and so will your students!

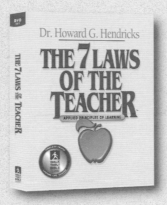

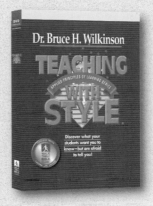

The 7 Laws of the Learner

Transform your teaching by understanding how students learn.

When you know how students learn, then you can teach so that students absorb, comprehend, and retain new information. You'll influence life-changing learning!

The 7 Laws of the Teacher

Learn what is needed to be a transformational teacher.

Having expertise doesn't mean you can effectively teach and transfer that knowledge to others. Learn what is needed to teach and to teach so well that you transform learning!

Teaching With Style

Transform your student's attentiveness and your effectiveness.

The #1 complaint about teachers is that they are boring. By understanding and applying simple principles, you'll never have a student say you weren't an engaging teacher!

Acclaimed by teachers and students alike, this classic Walk Thru the Bible teaching series has equipped teachers across the globe to better understand their students, teach in a way that transforms learning, and create a love for learning.

Buy the Set and Save $50!

Also available separately

---

www.walkthru.org/teachingseries or 1.800.361.6131

WALK THRU THE BIBLE

TAKE A WALK. CHANGE THE WORLD.

Profile of Style

1. WHO is TEACHING WITH STYLE for?

Teaching with Style is not just for teachers! Unless, of course, you would agree that everyone is a teacher at some time.

Perhaps you are a full-time teacher, instructor, or even a professor. *Teaching with Style* is definitely for you. But even if you don't teach professionally, this seminar will be of tremendous value.

Parents, pastors, camp counselors, volunteer teachers, Sunday school teachers, Bible study leaders—plus other group and organizational leaders—all have seen how much more effective their communication becomes when they do it with *STYLE!*

2. WHAT is TEACHING WITH STYLE?

A six-part course designed to eliminate the #1 worldwide hindrance to learning: BOREDOM!

This course is presented in one of two formats: video or live teaching sessions. Regardless of which you attend, you will never communicate or teach the same way again.

The Bible is the basis for *Teaching with Style* for two reasons:

1. Jesus Christ is universally acclaimed as history's most effective teacher.
2. The Bible is filled with examples of God's effective and creative communication with mankind.

Therefore, where better could we look for insight into communicating with STYLE than in the Scriptures—the record of God's creative revelation of Himself to mankind!

3. WHERE did TEACHING WITH STYLE originate?

Have you ever heard anyone say, "Jesus sure is a boring person!?"

Or how about this: "Wow! The Lord was really present in the church service tonight! But it was awfully boring."

You've probably never heard either! If God is never boring, why are His earthly ambassadors (teachers) not as equally dynamic?

That question in the heart of Dr. Bruce Wilkinson prompted a study lasting several years. The quest was to find what makes God such a powerful (NON-BORING!) communicator, and then teach people His methods.

The result? *Teaching with Style*!

4. WHEN can TEACHING WITH STYLE be used?

The live version of *Teaching with Style* is best for larger church groups (for example, a church-wide presentation) or denominational, organizational, or city-wide seminars.

The video format will be the most widely used because of its simplicity and efficiency. Any small group, Sunday school class, Christian school faculty, individual teacher, or others interested in improving their communication skills can now do so with ease and convenience.

5. WHY should you attend each session of TEACHING WITII STYLE?

Here's what will happen when you faithfully attend all six of the *Teaching with Style* sessions, live or video format:

- You will be awakened to the most vital need in teaching today.
- You will be taught the universal principles of style.
- You will learn the Biblical characteristics of style.
- You will discover how to possess the internal beliefs of style.
- You will learn to make your body your greatest teaching asset.
- You will see that anyone, regardless of personality type, can teach with style.
- You will learn how to use the same methods Christ did in His teaching.

6. HOW does the TEACHING WITH STYLE format work?

In each of the six sessions, your workbook will direct you through the following:
- Take notes on the session's content.
- "Discussion" questions to use with a group or on your own.
- Seven daily devotions taking you into the Scriptures for "style-study."
- A challenging set of projects: choose the right level for you.
- An opportunity to make a commitment to apply what you've learned in the session—to move ahead and Teach with Style!

UNIVERSAL PRINCIPLES

Great people live by
time-honored principles.
The same is true
of great teachers.
Are your principles
the Universal
Principles of Style?
There's one way to
find out—turn the page!

_____

_____

_____

_____

_____

PRINCIPLE 1

Style is the process by which the teacher delivers the subject to the _____.

_____

_____

_____

_____

PRINCIPLE 2

Style is the primary cause of student
_____ or _____.

_____

_____

_____

_____

PRINCIPLE 3

Style is the responsibility of the teacher and is within the teacher's complete _____ .

_____

_____

_____

PRINCIPLE 4

Style is influenced by personality but is controlled by the role the teacher _____ .

_____

_____

_____

PRINCIPLE 5

Style should be consciously planned according to the boundaries of the _____ ,
_____ , _____ , and _____ .

_____

_____

_____

PRINCIPLE 6

Style is fluid and must be adjusted according to the response of your _____ .

_____

_____

_____

_____

PRINCIPLE 7

Style is a learned skill and can be significantly improved through _____ and _____ .

_____

_____

_____

SESSION ONE CONCLUSION

_____

_____

_____

_____

Mastering the Minimum

What was the main point of this session? Try to capture in two to three sentences the "Big Idea." (Hint: what was the subject? What was said about the subject?)

_____

_____

_____

Perspectives on the Principles

Evaluate your teaching style below in light of the seven Universal Principles. (Record your score in the space.)

Never	Seldom	Sometimes	Usually	Always
1	2	3	4	5

1. I devote planning time in my lesson preparations to deciding which style will best deliver my content. (_____)

2. When my students seem bored, the first thing I check is the style I am using. (_____)

3. I practice the principle of deliberately choosing how I will act in class (vs. "just being myself"). (_____)

4. I consistently differ in my role as teacher from other roles in life I must fulfill. (_____)

5. In my lesson/content preparation, I evaluate subject, size, setting, and seniority before teaching. (_____)

6. I change styles easily while teaching based on the students' response to my content. (_____)

7. In the course of a year, I participate regularly in activities designed to increase my teaching skills. (_____)

Add up your total points and enter your score in the margin.

My score: [____]

30 – 35   Expert: making principles a priority!

25 – 29   Advanced: your students appreciate you!

20 – 24   Intermediate: could go either way!

15 – 19   Beginner: unclear on the concept!

10 – 14   Boring: what was the question?

A Person of Principles

Have you ever known a teacher or speaker who was low-key and reserved out of class but in class was a dynamo? Contrast this person's "everyday" personality with their teaching style:

Normally he or she is . . .

But in class he or she is . . .

Which principle from this session was the teacher implementing? (Rewrite the principle here in your own words.)

Are Your Principles Showing?

If your students thoroughly understood the seven Universal Principles, they would choose number _____ as being the principle most evident in your life.

They would choose number _____ as the one needing the most improvement.

Try to recall a student conversation or incident which led you to answer as you did above:

Planning to Practice the Principles

In the area you cited for improvement in D above, write down two steps you can take this week to make progress:

1. _____

2. _____

Develop a "Style" mindset daily as you discover from Scripture how the Universal Principles can make a difference—in your teaching! During the next several days, use the following practice exercises to apply what you learned in session one.

JUST BEGINNING

Reflect on some of your recent classes and write down what you think your students saw and heard when you taught. Describe your teaching style: voice, movement, variety, personality traits. Keep this self-portrait handy for review at the end of this course.

Interview the teacher or communicator with the most effective teaching style you know. Ask about style: history of successes and failures, disciplines he or she follows, how natural weaknesses were overcome, and how you might improve your own teaching style.

READY FOR A CHALLENGE

Purchase and study at least one book on effective teaching or communication style in the next six months. Make written notes on those points most applicable to your teaching, and implement them. Develop your own library of style resources for study.

Plan a one-month prayer focus on your own teaching ministry. Ask God for His insight and evaluation of your present level of commitment to teach with style and effectiveness. Renew your commitments to God in writing, and keep in a safe place for future review.

ADVANCED

Submit your teaching style to your peers for evaluation and improvement. Ask one fellow-teacher per month to evaluate your teaching style. Save the written report for comparison at a later date to note changes, progress, and other areas for improvement.

Involve your students in your quest to teach with effective style. Devise an anonymous questionnaire which they can fill out periodically on aspects of your teaching style: your personal traits, what's exciting, what's boring, progress made. Summarize and discuss.

The person who lays a foundation to teach with style knows that **style is the process by which a teacher delivers the subject to the student.** In fact, he or she knows that style will be the **primary cause of student boredom or excitement.** This teacher agrees that the **teacher is responsible** for style—it is **within his or her complete control.** While style **is influenced by personality,** it is determined by **the role the teacher selects. Subject, size, setting, and seniority** are conscious considerations in choosing a style. Additionally, style **is fluid and must be adjusted according to the response of the audience.** Are teachers-with-style born with style? No! They develop it over time, since **style is a learned skill and can be significantly improved through understanding and practice.**

The teacher who lays the foundation is a person who Teaches with Style! By the grace of God, you can be that person!

I **commit to Teach with Style through carefully laying the foundation— the foundation of universal principles which, when practiced, result in LifeChange in my students.**

_____

Signature/Date

Remember to read your __FREE__ Teaching With Style Daily Devotionals!
Visit www.walkthru.org/twsdevos to access the devotionals.

BIBLICAL
CHARACTERISTICS

When God communicates,
He captures everyone's
attention—big or small!
The characteristics of
His style are easy to
identify and to imitate.
But you have to know
what to look for
—and where!

_____

_____

_____

_____

_____

CHARACTERISTICS 1

God's style is _____.

_____

_____

_____

_____

CHARACTERISTICS 2

God's style is _____.

_____

_____

_____

_____

_____

CHARACTERISTICS 3

God's style is ———————————.

_____

_____

_____

_____

CHARACTERISTICS 4

God's style is ———————————.

_____

_____

_____

_____

CHARACTERISTICS 5

God's style is ———————————.

_____

_____

_____

_____

_____

CHARACTERISTICS 6

God's style is ———————————————————— .

_____

_____

_____

_____

CHARACTERISTICS 7

God's style is ———————————————————— .

_____

_____

_____

_____

SESSION TWO CONCLUSION

_____

_____

_____

_____

Mastering the Minimum

A fellow teacher misses this session due to illness. He calls the next day and says, "I'm in a hurry, but tell me—bottom line—what was the instructor's message?" Write your answer:

_____

_____

_____

A Characteristics Check-Up

Evaluate your teaching style below in light of the seven Biblical Characteristics. (Record your score in the space.)

Never	Seldom	Sometimes	Usually	Always
1	2	3	4	5

1. I take responsibility for the "memorability" of my content, not resting until I know my students have it.   (_____)

2. I am comfortable using "shock" treatment with my students to convey a point or get their attention.   (_____)

3. I use overhead projectors, film strips, videos, charts, graphs, maps, objects, and other visuals in my class.   (_____)

4. I prepare "one-time" teaching moments for my class which I know I will not repeat since they are unique.   (_____)

5. I plan learning experiences which utilize the senses of taste, touch, and smell as well as seeing and hearing.   (_____)

6. I consider it a personal goal to capture my students' attention and hold it from the beginning to the end of class. (_____)

7. I feel confident that I am a "living lecture" for my students; that my life illustrates the truths I teach.   (_____)

Add up your total points and enter your score in the margin.

My score: [_____]

30 – 35   Expert: making characteristics a priority!

25 – 29   Advanced: your students appreciate you!

20 – 24   Intermediate: could go either way!

15 – 19   Beginner: unclear on the concept!

10 – 14   Boring: what was the question?

A Captivating Characteristic

Jesus Christ is acknowledged by almost everyone to be the most captivating and effective teacher who ever lived. From your recollection of His ministry, what made His teaching style so captivating?

Who is the most captivating teacher you have ever heard? Compare his or her style to that of Jesus. What techniques did he or she use that were similar, or different? What kept you captivated?

What Are Your Characteristics?

If your students thoroughly understood the seven Biblical Characteristics, they would choose number _____ as being the characteristic most evident in your life.

They would choose number _____ as the one needing the most improvement.

Try to recall a student conversation or incident which led you to answer as you did above:

Make Your Characteristics Biblical!

What two things can you do in the immediate future to impact the area you cited for improvement in D above?

1.

2.

God's style is unexpected. These projects will help you do some unexpected things with YOUR students. During the next several days, use the following practice exercises to apply what you learned in session two.

JUST BEGINNING

Surprise your class by cancelling all scheduled activity for the day. Devote the time to your students: how they're doing, how they're feeling, what their concerns are in relation to class. Perhaps bring some refreshments to class for all to enjoy.

Give your students a copy of the next quiz or test you have planned. Tell them you want them all to make a "100"—that you're telling them now what they'll need to know to score perfectly. They'll be shocked, since most teachers want students to guess what's on the test!

READY FOR A CHALLENGE

Create an environment for learning by experience and identification. For instance, have the class wear blindfolds for half the day to experience the challenges of living as a blind person. Have them fast at lunch to understand hunger.

Bring to class facts, pictures, videos, music, magazines, and other supportive materials to shock your students with the reality of your content. Overwhelm them with data to drive home the point.

ADVANCED

Bring in a person who can deliver a dramatic rebuke to the class in an area of complacency: a law enforcement officer, a convict, a substance abuser. Have them speak firmly to the class in order to create a shock effect. Be sure to relieve any "pressure" that is created.

Reveal some aspect of your own life or background (or that of a well-known person whose background is public knowledge) unknown to the class which might surprise them. Do this carefully and appropriately, making the shock value support the point of the lesson.

The person who knows the Scriptures is a person who is becoming equipped to teach with style. When the teacher with God's style teaches, he or she will be remembered, since God's style is **memorable.** It is also **unexpected**—at times shocking students into a state of attentiveness—much as God did at times. God shocked not only by His words, but by His actions, since His style was not only verbal but **visual.** His style was anything but commonplace—it was often **unique**, only for one particular audience. Having captured their students' attention, teachers with style stretch them by making content **multisensory.** Teachers with style keep students' attention by being **captivating**. And they model content by being **incarnational**—showing as well as telling.

The person who knows the Scriptures is a person who Teaches with Style! By the grace of God, you can be that person!

God, who at various times and in different ways spoke in time past to the fathers by the prophets, has in these last days spoken to us by His Son . . . .

Hebrews 1:1-2

I **commit to Teach with Style through a growing knowledge of the Scriptures—that lifetime acquisition of the knowledge of God and His style, which, when practiced, results in LifeChange in my students.**

Signature / Date

Remember to read your <u>FREE</u> Teaching With Style Daily Devotionals!
Visit www.walkthru.org/twsdevos to access the devotionals.

INTERNAL
BELIEFS

Teaching with style
doesn't just happen.
Style is the overflow
of a heart burning
with the basics—
the basics which form
the basis of style.
Do you know what
they are?
You're about to
discover them
for yourself!

_____

_____

_____

_____

_____

BELIEF 1

Passion to _____ .

_____

_____

_____

_____

BELIEF 2

Love for _____ .

_____

_____

_____

_____

BELIEF 3

Sense of commission from _____ .

_____

_____

_____

_____

BELIEF 4

High degree of _____ .

1. _____   3. _____

2. _____   4. _____

_____

_____

BELIEF 5

Conviction of the message's

_____ .

_____

_____

_____

_____

BELIEF 6

Integrity with the ——————————.

_____

_____

_____

BELIEF 7

Dependence upon ——————————.

_____

_____

_____

_____

_____

SESSION THREE CONCLUSION

_____

_____

_____

_____

Mastering the Minimum

You've just returned home from Session Three. You record in your journal what you felt was the primary message of this session for any teacher. You enter today's date and write . . .

_____

_____

Focusing on Your Internal Beliefs

Evaluate your teaching style below in light of the seven Internal Beliefs. (Record your score in the space.)

Never	Seldom	Sometimes	Usually	Always
1	2	3	4	5

1. On any given day, those who observe me would quickly agree that teaching is my consuming passion.   (_____)

2. I develop close relationships and friendships among my students which go beyond class time.   (_____)

3. Whenever I teach, it is with a sense of purpose that God *wants* me to teach, that it is His will for me to do so.   (_____)

4. I arrive at my class time refreshed, confident, and well-versed having prepared my lessons in advance.   (_____)

5. Regardless of what content I teach, I am totally committed to the lifechanging potential of my lesson.   (_____)

6. My conscience remains clear as I teach because I practice the content I am communicating to others.   (_____)

7. I have a clear and practical understanding of how dependence upon God impacts the lesson I present.   (_____)

Add up your total points and enter your score in the margin.

My score: [_____]

30 – 35   Expert: making beliefs a priority!

25 – 29   Advanced: your students appreciate you!

20 – 24   Intermediate: could go either way!

15 – 19   Beginner: unclear on the concept!

10 – 14   Boring: what was the question?

A Barometer for Internal Beliefs

Internally, what is the difference between a teacher who is "recruited" vs. one who senses a "commission" from God to teach? What impact does one's internal sense of settledness and mission have on the way one teaches? Complete the sentences below:

I have known teachers who were recruited to teach because they were "available." I would describe their teaching as . . .

I have known other teachers who *know,* from the Lord, they are to teach their class. I would describe their teaching as . . .

Broadcasting Your Beliefs

If your students thoroughly understood the seven Internal Beliefs, they would choose number _____ as being the belief most evident in your life.

They would choose number _____ as the one needing the most improvement.

Try to recall a student conversation or incident which led you to answer as you did above:

Becoming a Belief-er

In the area you cited for improvement in D above, write down two steps you can take this week to make progress:

1. _____

2. _____

During the next several days, use the following practice exercises to apply what you learned in session three.

JUST BEGINNING

Plan to arrive at your teaching setting a half-hour early. Pray for particular students and their needs as you walk around the room. Pray that the Holy Spirit would protect the class from any kind of disruption and anoint it for lifechange.

Purchase several popular secular magazines written for your class' age or interest group. Pick out quotes, pictures, facts, interviews, or other items which you could use in your class to stimulate discussion and to compare with the Bible's perspective.

READY FOR A CHALLENGE

Call 3-5 students and tell them what your topic is for the next class. Ask for their suggestions, insights, and opinions and build their responses into your preparation. Consider having a student(s) participate in the class presentation with their own contribution.

Identify a week in advance the Scripture passages for your upcoming class content. Meditate on those Scriptures daily. Ask God to give you insights, illustrations, confirmations, and applications concerning those verses.

ADVANCED

Find people who have "experienced" the content you are teaching. Invite them to class and interview them: How did they learn the content? How did they apply it? What were the results? Would they recommend the truth you're presenting? What advice would they give?

Develop a partnership with a fellow teacher to hold one another accountable for early lesson preparation. Agree together on the amount of time you feel is adequate for your preparation, and when you plan to schedule that time. Check on one another regularly.

The person who teaches with style with a prepared heart has a **passion to communicate**—nothing can quench that desire! Passion is manifest in a **love for students**, and is borne out of a deep sense of **commission from God**. This teacher is doing the right thing by teaching—and knows it! He or she joyfully exercises the **high degree of preparation** needed to creatively teach the lesson. The necessary time is invested because this teacher is so utterly **convicted of the message's power**. There is power in content, but even more power in a life which demonstrates the truth. Therefore, the teacher with a prepared heart has **integrity with the message**. This teacher is humble enough to realize that without **dependence upon God**, no teaching will have its maximum impact.

The person whose heart is prepared is a person who Teaches with Style! By the grace of God, you can be that person!

I **commit to Teach with Style through the continuing preparation of my heart—the nurturing of those internal beliefs which, when practiced, result in LifeChange in my students.**

Signature / Date

Remember to read your FREE Teaching With Style Daily Devotionals!
Visit www.walkthru.org/twsdevos to access the devotionals.

EXTERNAL
BEHAVIORS

What causes teachers' feet
to freeze to the floor,
their hands to lock on the
podium, their mouth to
fill with cotton, and
butterflies to swarm
in their stomach?
In this session
you'll discover how
to make your body
your best teaching tool.
So relax—and enjoy!

BEHAVIORS 1

BEHAVIORS 2

BEHAVIORS 3

_____

BEHAVIORS 4

_____

BEHAVIORS 5

_____

BEHAVIORS 6

_____

BEHAVIORS 7

_____

Mastering the Minimum

The morning after attending Session Four, you're looking in the mirror preparing for the day. The main point of the message about the use of your body in teaching is still on your mind . . .

Looking for Boring Behaviors

Evaluate your teaching style below in light of the seven External Behaviors. (Record your score in the space.)

Never	Seldom	Sometimes	Usually	Always
1	2	3	4	5

1. My voice varies in pitch, volume, and intensity when I teach, either naturally or through deliberate effort.   (_____)

2. I speak for extended periods of time in direct eye contact with my students, even when lecturing.   (_____)

3. I am conscious of deliberately changing the expressions on my face a number of times during my class.   (_____)

4. My hands and arms are comfortable pointers, illustrators, and attention-keepers when I teach.   (_____)

5. I bend, sit, twist, stretch, and use any other body language available and appropriate when I teach.   (_____)

6. Appearance is a consistent consideration when I plan my teaching sessions, and I vary it accordingly.   (_____)

7. Over the course of a class session, I move in and out of all "four corners" of my classroom or teaching area.   (_____)

Add up your total points and enter your score in the margin.

My score: [_____]

30 – 35   **Expert:** making behaviors a priority!

25 – 29   **Advanced:** your students appreciate you!

20 – 24   **Intermediate:** could go either way!

15 – 19   **Beginner:** unclear on the concept!

10 – 14   **Boring:** what was the question?

Building on Others' Behaviors

Think for a moment about teachers or communicators you have heard. Picture those for whom the external dimensions of teaching were a primary asset, and those who did not use their physical abilities to maximum potential.

From the teacher who used physical style well, I would love to learn how to . . .

Watching the speaker who did not use physical style well makes me want to avoid . . .

Preparing to Change Some Behaviors

If your students thoroughly understood the seven External Behaviors, they would choose number _____ as being the behavior most evident in your life.

They would choose number _____ as the one needing the most improvement.

Try to recall a student conversation or incident which led you to answer as you did above:

Banishing Boredom from Behaviors

In the area you cited for improvement in D above, write down two steps you can take this week to make progress:

1. _____

2. _____

PRACTICING EXTERNAL BEHAVIORS

During the next several days, use the following practice exercises to apply what you learned in session four.

JUST BEGINNING

Read a familiar children's story out loud such as "Casey At the Bat" or "The Three Little Pigs" with exaggerated gestures. Better yet, read it to a group of children and lead them in doing the gestures and motions with you!

Practice gesturing in front of a mirror every night for a month. Exaggerate all of your gestures—just to get used to feeling your hands and arms moving in different ways. Work with all three dimensions spatially: height, breadth, and depth.

READY FOR A CHALLENGE

Ask a friend to observe your teaching and fill out a gesture grid like the one in the Appendix of this workbook. Have your friend mark every time you gesture. Mark the ranges vertically, horizontally, and in terms of depth. Repeat in six months to measure progress.

Build into your lesson plan places to use large gestures: how wide or tall something is; a shocking emotional description; pointing toward the horizon or heaven; hands on hips or knees in mock amazement. Making plans ahead of time increases your security.

ADVANCED

Observe a teacher who enjoys great freedom of movement with his or her arms and hands while speaking. Evaluate this speaker's gestures with a gesture grid (see #3 above). Compare your gestures with those of the teacher you observed. How can you improve?

Video tape your class so as to watch your gestures. Most teachers don't believe how little they gesture until they see themselves on video. Also video tape yourself practice-teaching at home. Review the tape and critique yourself, noting areas needing improvement.

The person who defeats the giants of Intimidation and Inhibition to teach with style has made a commitment to teach regardless of the cost. The teacher with style knows that the **voice** which never varies is the single greatest cause of boredom in the classroom. This teacher also knows that **eye** contact with students says more than many words—and that an expressive **face** communicates a whole range of powerful emotions. **Gestures**—the most intimidating use of the body—give teachers a second voice with which to teach. The teacher with style combines all of these with a **posture** suitable for the point, and an **appearance** suitable for the audience. Having prepared in this way, the teacher with style uses **movement** to carry the content to the student.

The person who defeats the giants is a person who Teaches with Style! By the grace of God, you can be that person!

For God has not given us a spirit of fear, but of power and of love and of a sound mind.

2 Timothy 1:7

I **commit to Teach with Style through defeating the giants of Intimidation and Inhibition—the commitment to use my body to serve my students, which, when practiced, results in LifeChange in my students.**

_____

Signature / Date

Remember to read your FREE Teaching With Style Daily Devotionals!
Visit www.walkthru.org/twsdevos to access the devotionals.

YOUR
PERSONALITY

Personality—
every teacher has one!
The critical issue is not
"what kind?" but "what style?"
Regardless of your
personality type, using
energy, variety, emotion,
and other style intangibles
can put your class in the
palm of your . . . personality!
So grab a smile and
let's begin!

_____

_____

_____

_____

_____

_____

PERSONALITY 1

_____

_____

_____

_____

_____

_____

PERSONALITY 2

_____

1. _____   2. _____

_____

_____

_____

_____

PERSONALITY 3

_____

1. _____

2. _____

3. _____

4. _____

PERSONALITY 4

_____

1. _____

2. _____

3. _____

PERSONALITY 5

_____

PERSONALITY 6

_____

PERSONALITY 7

_____

1. _____
2. _____
3. _____
4. _____

SESSION FIVE CONCLUSION

Mastering the Minimum

People and their personalities can be a sensitive issue. What is the central truth you learned in this session which gives you freedom to maximize your personality in teaching?

Perspectives on Your Personality

Evaluate your teaching style below in light of the seven Personality traits in Session Five. (Record your score in the space.)

Never	Seldom	Sometimes	Usually	Always
1	2	3	4	5

1. I maintain a high energy level in my class to hold attention, either by choice or by natural teaching style.   (____)

2. I use variety in my personality (moods and expressions) to complement my content and teaching points.   (____)

3. My students and I have regular "below-the-surface" exchanges in class in which personal issues are shared.   (____)

4. Planned and confident use of humor—as part of my lesson plan—is a consistent aspect of my style.   (____)

5. Expressing emotional intensity to highlight or illustrate teaching points is within my "comfort zone."   (____)

6. My students would tell you that I am a "creative" teacher in terms of content presentation and application.   (____)

7. My personality reveals my high motivation to teach; in return, my students are motivated to learn.   (____)

Add up your total points and enter your score in the margin.

My score: [____]

30 – 35   Expert: making personality a priority!

25 – 29   Advanced: your students appreciate you!

20 – 24   Intermediate: could go either way!

15 – 19   Beginner: unclear on the concept!

10 – 14   Boring: what was the question?

Personalities in Your Past

The seven traits identified in this session are those which make teaching more effective—because they help to hold attention and overcome boredom!

Think of a teacher in your past experience who exemplified one of the traits discussed in this session. Record here the person, the trait, and how that trait specifically impacted your learning experience— how that trait helped overcome boredom.

Your Personality and the Polls

If your students thoroughly understood the seven Personality traits, they would choose number _____ as being the trait most evident in your life.

They would choose number _____ as the one needing the most improvement.

Try to recall a student conversation or incident which led you to answer as you did above:

Personality and Practice

In the area you cited for improvement in D above, write down two steps you can take this week to make progress:

1. _____

2. _____

During the next several days, use the following practice exercises to apply what you learned in session five.

JUST BEGINNING

Reverse the order of the events in your teaching time. Whatever normal routine you follow, do the opposite. The point here is not confusion, but attention focused by variety. When students don't know what's "next," they pay closer attention.

Alter the proportion of time spent on activities in class. Give the largest proportion of time to whatever activity normally gets the least amount. For instance, calling roll: do mini-autobiographies as you call each name, helping students get to know each other better.

READY FOR A CHALLENGE

Arrange for a guest lecturer or substitute teacher to take your class for a day or period. But don't leave! Stay and participate, adding variety through having a different speaker whom your students are not used to (make sure your guest teaches with style!).

Rearrange your class room regularly—but not predictably! It is even more attention-holding to arrange your class on the basis of variety in teaching: work groups, discussion groups, lecture, debate, or other method.

ADVANCED

Cast a group of friends as "actors" who will teach the bulk of your content through dramas, role plays, dramatic monologues, skits, or other dramatic methods. "Stage" a dramatic event which your students don't know is fabricated to make a teaching point; then explain.

Take your students to a different location for the class session. Arrange transportation and adhere to schedules so as not to cause inconvenience. Make it a surprise until you get there. Have the students evaluate the impact of the change in setting.

The person who teaches with style moves beyond the limits of his or her natural style of teaching. An **energy** level is present which is contagious. Students respond and are kept on the edge of attentiveness by the **variety** used—always a new look, a new plan, a new adventure in learning. Teachers with style promote openness and sharing by employing **transparency**—and then balancing serious moments with healthy doses of **humor. Emotions**, and their liberal and timely expression, are a prerequisite for teaching with style. Undergirding all other personality skills is **creativity:** mixing just the right blend of personality and style. The end result? **Motivation,** that priceless treasure that moves students beyond today into tomorrow.

The person who doesn't act naturally is a person who Teaches with Style! By the grace of God, you can be that person!

I commit to Teach with Style through moving beyond my natural style—to use my personality in genuine and creative ways, which, when implemented, result in LifeChange in my students.

Signature/Date

Remember to read your <u>FREE</u> *Teaching With Style Daily Devotionals!*
Visit www.walkthru.org/twsdevos to access the devotionals.

GREAT
METHODOLOGY

To know what makes
great methodology,
you have to ask a
Great Teacher—
like Jesus Christ.
In this session
you'll discover some
startling facts about
the methods
Christ used, and why.
And best of all,
you'll learn how
you can teach like Him—
using His methods!

_____

_____

_____

_____

_____

METHODOLOGY 1

_____

_____

_____

_____

_____

METHODOLOGY 2

_____   _____

_____

1. _____   3. _____

2. _____   4. _____

_____

_____

METHODOLOGY 3

_____ _____

METHODOLOGY 4

_____ ____ _____

METHODOLOGY 5

_____

METHODOLOGY6

_____

METHODOLOGY 7

_____

Mastering the Minimum

You're discussing methodology with a teacher who didn't attend Teaching with Style. Your friend doesn't believe methods make that much difference. What is your one-sentence response?

Measuring <u>Your</u> Methodology

Evaluate your teaching style below in light of the seven Methodologies. (Record your score in the space.)

Never	Seldom	Sometimes	Usually	Always
1	2	3	4	5

1. When I lecture, it is by choice, not from lack of planning; I use lecture because it accomplishes a specific goal.   (_____)

2. The majority of the stories I tell as illustrations are of my own creation.   (_____)

3. In every class I teach, I introduce a visual aid of some kind, even if it is just painting a detailed word picture.   (_____)

4. When students ask questions, I answer with a question to lead them in self-discovery of the truth.   (_____)

5. The discussions which take place in my class are as a result of planning as well as spontaneous ones.   (_____)

6. Drama, role play, dramatic readings, skits, and scripted plays are part of my teaching methodology.   (_____)

7. I assign out-of-class projects to my students to reinforce what I have been teaching in class.   (_____)

Add up your total points and enter your score in the margin.

My score: [____]

30 – 35   Expert: making methods a priority!

25 – 29   Advanced: your students appreciate you!

20 – 24   Intermediate: could go either way!

15 – 19   Beginner: unclear on the concept!

10 – 14   Boring: what was the question?

Masters of Methods

Some teachers seem to excel at one or two particular teaching methods—perhaps stories, maybe drama. Think about two teachers you have seen who were masters of their methodology—they had made a fine art out of a method.

One teacher used _____ more effectively than any teacher I've ever seen by . . .

_____

Another teacher was a master at _____ . He or she would astound us by . . .

_____

Your Most-Noticed Methods

If your students thoroughly understood the seven Methodologies, they would choose number _____ as being the one most evident in your life.

They would choose number _____ as the method most needing improvement.

Try to recall a student conversation or incident which led you to answer as you did above:

_____

Moving Toward More Methodology

In the area you cited for improvement in D above, write down two steps you can take this week to make progress:

1. _____

2. _____

During the next several days, use the following practice exercises to apply what you learned in session six.

JUST BEGINNING

Take your class to see what you are teaching about. If it's government, go to the courthouse or capital. If it's disease, go to the hospital. If it's history, go to a museum. Show them in person the thing or concept you are talking about in class.

Assign your students the responsibility for creating visual aids to illustrate and support an upcoming class topic. Make sure they have materials and skills to accomplish the task. Save the visual aids over the length of the class for display.

READY FOR A CHALLENGE

Inventory the visual aids you use in teaching: pictures, objects, videos, on-site inspections, charts, maps, overhead transparencies, movies, TV programs, magazines, books. Keep a record of when you used each aid so as to insure variety and future use.

Invite an authority to come to your class who teaches by visual demonstration rather than lecture. Observe the attention and retention level of your students during and after. Give your students a quiz to measure their retention through visual observation.

ADVANCED

Create a visual aids center in your classroom to promote students' creation and use of visual aids in their assignments and projects. When they are responsible for reports or presentations, require visual aids based on the equipment you make available.

Teach your students discernment through a study of the media's use of visual aids in communicating subliminal messages through various methods. Bring in samples and discuss the spiritual and emotional power of the visual media.

The teacher who models his or her teaching methods after those of Christ is a teacher who teaches with style. Christ taught with authority, and no more so than when He delivered a **lecture.** As He gave the truth, He illustrated that truth with **stories** from life. He was able to teach wherever He went, because He always had **visual aids** at hand. To promote self-learning and deep thinking, Christ used **questions and answers** to pull His "students" along in their discovery of truth. And when those questions raised difficult issues, He was more likely to promote a **discussion** than solve the dilemma outright. And **drama!** Christ loved it, because it pictured truth in an unforgettable way. Christ also assigned **projects** so the disciples could put the truth to work.

The person who teaches like Christ is a person who Teaches with Style! By the grace of God, you can be that person!

I **commit to Teach with Style through following the methodology of Christ—the practice of dynamic methods which, when used, result in LifeChange in my students.**

_____

Signature / Date

Remember to read your __FREE__ Teaching With Style Daily Devotionals!
Visit www.walkthru.org/twsdevos to access the devotionals.

DIAGNOSTIC
CHARTS

The last point in Session One on Universal Principles of Style says that "Style is a learned skill and can be significantly improved through understanding and practice." Now that you have understanding, it's time to practice—with Style!

Practice Makes Perfect!

The four charts to which you were introduced in Session Four (External Behaviors), are reproduced on the following pages for your use. Ask a friend or fellow-teacher to help you by recording your gestures, voice, and body and eye movements on the charts. In order to measure your progress, have someone fill out a set of charts on your style periodically, perhaps four times a year. Then compare the charts for progress and to note persistent "trouble spots." Learning new skills is much more enjoyable when progress is recorded, viewed, and appreciated over a significant length of time!

Permission Granted!

Walk Thru the Bible grants the owner of this Course Workbook permission to unlimited reproduction of these charts (pages A-2 through A-5) for diagnostic evaluations of his or her personal teaching style. Please do not reproduce otherwise.

Voice Chart

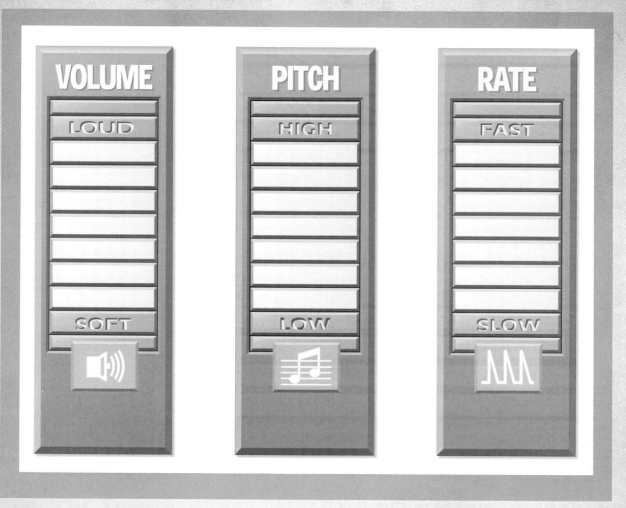

NOTE: Variation, or voice movement within the scales, is the ideal use of the voice.

To the Evaluator: After a few moments of listening, shade in the horizontal panel on each of the three gauges indicating where the speaker's volume, pitch, and rate "stays" most of the time. Then place individual dots above and below the "normal" panel to indicate each time the speaker diverts above or below the norm, and to what degree.

Eyes Chart

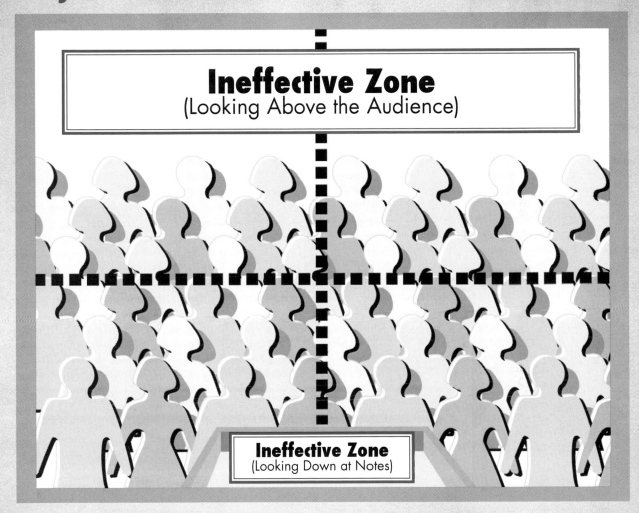

Ineffective Zone
(Looking Above the Audience)

Ineffective Zone
(Looking Down at Notes)

NOTE: Avoid the "Ineffective Zones" by talking to the four quadrants of your audience.

To the Evaluator: From your vantage point in the audience, watch the speaker's eyes. Indicate with small check marks on this chart the faces where he or she focuses (be sure and indicate if the speaker's eyes stay in the Ineffective Zones). If the speaker uses the helpful technique of making and holding eye contact with an audience member for an extended time (15-20 seconds), draw a circle around a figure to represent that extended contact.

Gestures Chart

**NOTE: Gestures should extend into all three spatial
dimensions: height, width, and depth.**

To the Evaluator: Indicate with a dot or small check each time a
significant gesture is made, showing both the area and the degree of
extension. Upon completion of the teaching session, use circles to group
clusters of marks to show patterns and tendencies and to highlight
"unused" areas. Clusters of marks close to the body indicate a need for
practicing extension of the hands and arms.

Movement Chart

NOTE: Movement should be coupled with timing
and mood for maximum effectiveness.

To the Evaluator: The Movement Chart tracks the speaker's extent of mobility and mood when teaching. Write words such as "normal," "excited," "serious," "humorous," "story," and other mood or activity indicators on the chart <u>in the location where the speaker was when conveying that information or mood</u>. Use check marks next to the words to indicate multiple instances of the same movement and mood combinations. Assess afterwards for the best combinations: behind the podium for lecture, near the audience for humor, rapid movement for exciting content, etc.

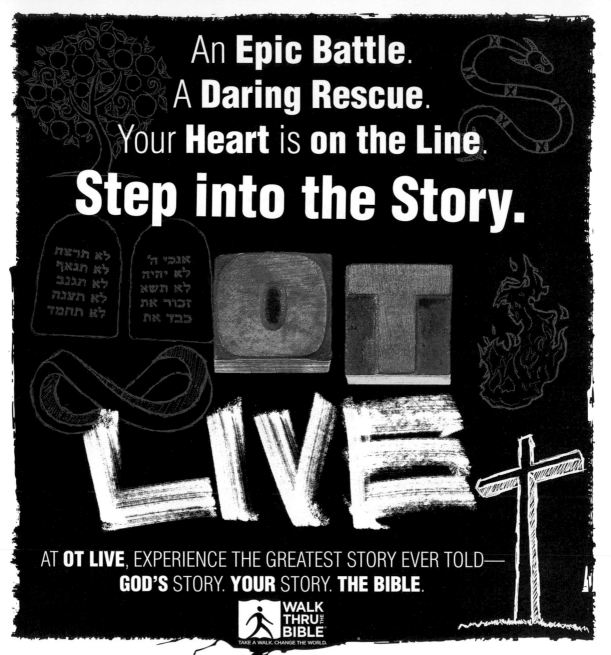

An **Epic Battle**.
A **Daring Rescue**.
Your **Heart** is **on the Line**.

Step into the Story.

AT **OT LIVE**, EXPERIENCE THE GREATEST STORY EVER TOLD—
GOD'S STORY. **YOUR** STORY. **THE BIBLE.**

WALK THRU THE BIBLE®
TAKE A WALK. CHANGE THE WORLD.

A Live Event with an Eternal Impact.
Walk Thru the Bible events unfold the big picture of the Bible in a way
you've never EVER experienced!

- Learn in a few hours what would have taken months to discover!
- Remove the intimidation factor from the Bible!
- Realize learning the Bible can be fun and exciting!
- Be able to read the Bible and understand the story!

Host a live event in your church, school, or organization.
Live events available for children, students, & adults.

www.walkthru.org/live-events

Walk Thru the Bible
Magazine Rack

Closer Walk Reading Scripture reveals what God says about Himself and what He has to say about you—His plans and purpose for you. *Closer Walk* is a daily devotional guide, accompanied by excerpts from great teachers of the faith, for reading through the entire New Testament in one year.

Daily Walk God speaks every day!
Are you listening? Unique insights, overviews, charts, and other special features have made *Daily Walk* a dependable Bible study tool for over 25 years. With its systematic reading plan, your life will be revolutionized as you read through the entire Bible in just one year.

Tapestry *Weaving God's Wisdom into a Woman's Heart.* Just as one tapestry's delicate beauty is different from another, your relationship with God is unique and unduplicated. *Tapestry* draws you into His presence
and offers guidance, encouragement, and a realistic presentation of what it means to be a Christian woman in today's complex world.

indeed *Exploring the Heart of God.*
If you desire to know God's heart more deeply, *indeed* is the devotional you want. By focusing on one short passage each day, new insights and new applications are revealed that show your part in God's great plan. For those who want to meditate deeply on the wisdom of Scripture, *indeed* will help you mine those treasures.

YW is a magazine of daily devotionals designed to help students navigate the Bible, to get to know God through it, and to answer His call to live the adventure. This adventure, stamped by the Holy Spirit and pioneered by Jesus Christ, is dangerous yet wonderful, day-to-day yet holy. Invite your students to step into the journey with us.

To order, visit our website:
www.devotionals.org